Cheap Railways: A Letter To The People Of Bruce And Grey

George Laidlaw

In the interest of creating a more extensive selection of rare historical book reprints, we have chosen to reproduce this title even though it may possibly have occasional imperfections such as missing and blurred pages, missing text, poor pictures, markings, dark backgrounds and other reproduction issues beyond our control. Because this work is culturally important, we have made it available as a part of our commitment to protecting, preserving and promoting the world's literature. Thank you for your understanding.

CHEAP RAILWAYS.

A LETTER

TO THE PEOPLE OF

BRUCE AND GREY,

SHOWING THE

Advantages, Practicability and Cost

OF A

CHEAP RAILWAY FROM TORONTO

THROUGH THESE COUNTIES;

WITH AN APPENDIX ADDRESSED TO THE PEOPLE
OF ONTARIO AND VICTORIA.

By GEORGE LAIDLAW.

TORONTO:
GLOBE PRINTING COMPANY, 26 & 28 KING STREET EAST.
1867.

To the Wardens of Bruce and Grey,
  the Mayor of Owen Sound, and
    the Farmers on the Route of the Proposed
      Central Railway.

GENTLEMEN,—

I beg leave most respectfully to submit, for your consideration, reasons why you should heartily and energetically support the immediate construction of a railway direct to Toronto, in preference to one on any other route; and will endeavour to show that the railway should be built on the cheap light narrow gauge principle, such as cost in one instance, in Australia, about £2,100 Sterling per mile, and which paid the first year 8 per cent. dividend.

These kind of railways give great satisfaction in Norway, a country similar to Canada in climate and productions, but presenting many difficulties to the construction of cheap railways, being so mountainous and rugged. The distance of your counties from the leading markets renders unprofitable the cultivation of a surplus over local wants, of barley, peas, oats and roots.

The average price of these articles rules so low, that they won't generally pay reasonable cost for production, and heavy charges for freight to remote markets. Wheat, pork, butter and ashes, being greater value in less bulk, bear heavy charges for freight better than the coarser kinds of farm and forest produce. Observe, the bulk of your wheat is bought in winter, for less than its relative value, because it cannot be moved until spring, and has to be held a long time, subject to heavy charges for interest, insurance and storage—a loss further augmented by the caution of Bankers and Dealers, who require and will have plenty of margin to cover such long risks.

These circumstances diminish competition. The bug-bear which retards the settlement of our wild lands, and the rock which diverts from our favoured country the current of emigration, is the timber, which for want of freight you are compelled to destroy, at a cost in labour of about $14 an acre. Your summer sky is darkened with the smoke of burning money, while elm and oak are worth in Quebec 1s. 3d. to 1s. 9d. a cubic foot, and pine lumber in Toronto $10, $16, $20, as in quality.

Yourselves and families labour with weary limbs to log up and burn your beech and maple, while the citizens of Toronto are paying $7 50 per cord, and cartage, for fuel, and those who cannot buy a cord at a time, pay 3d. per stick for what will cook their food and keep death by cold from their hearths. In this city, there is consumed annually about 350,000 dollars' worth of cordwood, and imported coals to the value of $200,000. A decrease in the price of cordwood to $4 50, or even $5, would probably change in your favour the disbursement of half that large amount, if you had a railway worked in favour of local interests, and *bound* by *law* to carry cordwood.

Picture the value, to the farmers on the Central Route, of a market at each station for fuel for the railway, and for the city of Toronto, where $1¾ to $2 in cash could be had for every cord! An engine, twelve cars and three or four men, at $2½ per cord freight, would gross on the Central light narrow gauge railway $110 per diem.

This trade would profit Upper Canada more than carrying Chicago flour to Boston, at rates charged for flour manufactured in the county of York.

The loss is incalculable to the districts traversed by the G. W. R., G. T. R., and N. R., because these roads have not afforded facilities for the conversion of cordwood into money, and consequently, now unbroken wilds into green fields. The increase of traffic would have more than repaid any advance in the cost of the fuel for their engines. The people, by legislation, ought to compel these railway companies, yet, to carry cordwood, on an equitable basis; it is vexatious to see how they strain after through traffic, for the benefit of our unneighbourly neighbours, who legislate with such vindicative hostility to our interests.

About 40,000 cords of wood were exported to Charlotte for fuel for the N. Y. Central Railway last season, that influential Corporation having secured a reduction of the duty. Proper facilities being afforded for carrying on this trade, it would largely increase. The competition engendered by it, and the exhaustion of supplies near navigable water, are the causes of the present high prices of cordwood.

The "yearly chopping" of your counties, sold at $1 50 to $2 per cord, would bring more money, *low transport being available, than all your crop of cereals, excepting wheat,* much as you may be surprised at the statement. Bush land in the front townships, near navigable water, is now more valuable than old cleared land; and this would be the case with land near railroads, if they would carry wood at fair rates.

In new settlements, a market for timber of all kinds—lumber, staves, shingles, hoops, bark, and fencing stuffs—is of paramount importance, as by this means the struggling farmers are enabled to *cash their labour,* and with the money obtained provide themselves with household necessities, seed, cattle &c., which are obtained with great difficulty when the first crops on the new clearings fail, from any cause, to meet the requirements of the case.

In the State of Maine, some railways have little or no other kind of traffic than the carriage of lumber, wood and bark.

The Grand Trunk Railway, east of this city, was built prematurely, in fact never should have been constructed lengthwise with the St. Lawrence, which does not require many repairs. The paddles dont wear, if they vex, its waters.

If a Grand Trunk line had to be built, it should have traversed the interior. Could the G. T. R. be cut up in pieces 100 miles long, and "upended," terminating each piece on the water front, then, with the aid of free grants of land to actual settlers, we should have breadth as well as length to this great country.

The counties west of Toronto are now harrassed, *during sleighing time particularly*, by extortionate rates of freight, being levied to keep life in parts of the line where no line should be. The G.T.R. charges about 40 *per cent.* on the produce of all the country it traverses west, over what the rates of freight *ought to be*, to Toronto, the nearest and best market in summer, because the best shipping port in all U. C. to all the southern and eastern markets.

To rivet the fetters of the G.T.R. more securely on the county of Bruce and part of Grey, it is unblushingly proposed and advocated by those whose discernment of your true interests is obscured by the patronage or influence of the G. T. R. Co., to construct a railway from Saugeen, or other point in Bruce, to Seaforth or Stratford. It is also proposed, with scarcely less effrontery, in the interest of the N. R., to build a line from Angus to Durham, or Walkerton.

These two propositions are the most grasping and selfish attempts conceivable on the part of these two railway corporations, to put their yoke on the necks of the people of Bruce and Grey.

We have got through with Jackson, Peto, Brassy and Betts, who know how to manipulate parliaments, municipalities, stocks, sub-contractors, &c., and you and the citizens of Toronto must take care and not fall victims to their clumsy successors, though not less avaricious imitators.

We have had enough of political contracts, plundering, humbugging of municipalities, (Toronto is out about $2,000,000, principal and interest) and money irretrievably sunk below the hope of dividends, and the well-known sequel—a few enriched and many fleeced.

The "raid" of the G. T. R. contractors costs Canada, per annum, over what it ought—more than the last year's raids of those rascally Fenians.

We ought to manage our new works in accordance with our resources, as manufacturers or merchants begin business in proportion to *their means and markets.*

The Railway from Durham to Angus would undoubtedly benefit the district traversed, but it would not benefit Grey to the extent of half the advantage to be derived from a Railway on the Central Route, which would be untramelled by any other policy than the *best* for the local interests *it will be built to serve.*

I see no reason why Bruce, Western and Northern Grey, should come under a mortgage to pay 40 per cent. excess of freight on the products of their industry, in the shape of a perennial freight tax, to either the proposed Durham branch of the N. R. R. or the Saugeen branch of the G. T. R. The money voted to assist the construction of these roads would only be a fractional part of the yearly lien of these roads on the industry of the districts tributary to them, and not half the benefits would accrue to your counties from these branches as from an independent line, worked in the interests of your counties and the trade of this city, both interests being fully identical on this question.

The people of Canada will sooner or later have to take such action as will protect them from being mere "counters" in the calculation of our Railroad managers. Many of the United States are groaning under railroad tyranny, and some of them, as will be seen from the subjoined extract, are endeavouring to emancipate themselves. The Titusville *Herald* says:

"A committee of the Ohio State Senate has been engaged in overhauling the management of railroads, express companies and telegraph companies. The results of its labours are embodied in a report, containing various recommendations, and in two bills containing such provisions as are necessary to carry out the conclusions to which they have come. They recommend that no railroad company shall be permitted to charge more for a shorter distance than for a longer one; that every company shall publish its tariff of rates and shall adhere to them, and be prohibited under penalties from allowing reductions from it to individual shippers or classes of shippers, and that preference in transportation shall be prohibited, except such as are allowed to live stock, perishable freight, and the like. The committee condemn the policy of freight and express companies having portions of their stock in the hands of railroad officers, and declare that agents and officers of every grade deal with the roads, accept offices and employments inconsistent with their duties, and engage in business which interferes with the rights of the general public. The employment of station agents by express companies is censured, as tending to interfere with the rights of the public in the carrying of baggage and parcels on passenger trains, with the interest of the road in its freight traffic, and with the rights of competing express companies. Finally, it is recommended that there shall be appointed a Commissioner of Railways, who shall be charged with the duty of collecting the statistics and the experience of railroad management in the State; of observing its immediate wants and defects; of attending to the enforcement of the law against railroad corporations, and of examining into abuses in railroad affairs, with the view of protecting the rights of the stockholders and of the public."

Toronto is indebted for its pre-eminence as the commercial capital of Upper Canada to its excellent harbour, and the extent and fertility of the country northwards. It is the best market, because the best distributing point for all that part of the peninsula north-west, north, and north-east of it. Freights from Toronto to Oswego, Kingston, Cape Vincent, Ogdensburg, and out to seaward, are cheaper, on account of its excellent harbour and other facilities of the port, *than from any other point on the north shore of Lake Ontario.*

These advantages redound to the benefit of all the people who here seek a shipping port or a market. If the rates of freight from all points east of Sarnia and Goderich, to Toronto, were fixed at the same rates as charged from these points to Montreal, Quebec, or Portland, then this city, by virtue of its position and facilities, would receive and re-ship to other markets, by water or rail, as might suit the interests of the holders (identical with those of the producer) all the products of the districts tributary to the G. T. R. west, better markets often being attainable, at less cost for freight, than those on the line of that road.

The cheapest road to the best markets is what you want to find, and having found, it is your interest to support the *establishment* of that route, with all your financial, municipal, and political strength.

That route is the Central, on the light narrow gauge system, and Toronto is the market. You know the latter fact already, and the other two we will endeavour to show you. Subjoined you have a table of the rates of freight to which your produce would be subject *via* the branch roads, at the rates charged by the G. T. R. and the N. R. for equal distances.

If they made the rates less than those stated on the branch roads, then the difference would be lost to the stockholders of the branches, which possibly would not disturb the other companies.

TABLE OF DISTANCES.

Toronto to Walkerton..............................95 miles, air-line.
Angus to Walkerton............... ....65 " "
Toronto to Angus................53 miles, air-line, 73 by N.R.R.
Walkerton to Seaforth...........................41 miles, air-line.
Toronto to Seaforth.............................113 miles by G. T. R.

Freight from Walkerton to Angus, as per rates charged by N.R.R.	From Angus to Toronto, as per tariff.	Total Freight Walkerton to Toronto, via Angus.
Lumber per car...$16 50	......$16 50......	......$33 00......
Staves " 16 50	...... 16 50......	...... 33 00......
Live Stock "....... 28 00	...... 29 00......	...... 57 00......
Cordwood (not carried.)		
Flour, per Brl.... 0 27	...... 0 28......	...... 0 55......
Grain, per Bush. 60 lbs............ 0 7½	...... 0 7½.....	...... 0 15......
Goods per ton, 3rd class............. 3 80	...... 4 00......	...... 7 80......

Freight to Seaforth from Walkerton, as per rates charged by G.T.R. to Toronto all *sleighing time*.	From Seaforth to Toronto, as per tariff, for the *sleighing time*.	Total Freight, Walkerton to Toronto, *via* Seaforth.
Lumber per car...$13 50	......$21 00......	......$34 50......
Staves " 13 50	...... 21 00......	...... 34 50......
Live Stock" 14 50	...... 27 00......	...... 41 50......
Cordwood (not carried.)		
Flour, per Brl.... 0 20	...... 0 33......	...... 0 53......
Grain, per Bush. 60 lbs............ 0 06	...... 0 10......	...... 0 16......
Goods, per ton, 3d class............... 2 60	...... 4 20......	...... 6 80......

Contrast this with the charges on the direct or central route from Walkerton to Toronto, at the same rate of freight per mile as the G. T. R. charges from Seaforth to Toronto,

FREIGHT—WALKERTON TO TORONTO.

Lumber (per car) $17 50
Live Stock   " 22 70
Flour (per Brl.).. 0 27½
Grain (per Bush. of 60 lbs.).............................. 0 8½
Goods (per ton, 3rd Class)................................ 3 53
Cordwood, Lumber Rates, (per cord.)................ 2 50
Staves, (per car) 17 50

In considering the foregoing statement and tables, you will see that trade is diverted from its natural channel and markets by the irresponsible and arbitrary fiats of gentlemen who necessarily study and carry out a policy favourable to the interests of their English employers, however disadvantageous that policy may be to the interests of the districts affected, or damaging to the prosperity of the capital of this Province. One-fifth of the rolling stock now employed in carrying to the eastern termini of the G. T. R., would bring to this city from the western sections G. T. R., at fair rates, all the produce, timber, cordwood, &c., destined for consumption in this or intermediate markets. If other sections of the G. T. R. fail to pay expenses, is it the fault of yourselves and neighbours, that you have to make good the loss?

The G. T. R. Company like to load their cars at the western termini and run them through at round freights to the other termini—Quebec or Portland—and reload for the same journey backwards, which is no doubt for the advantage of the Company, but is very far from being for the true interests of the farmers west of Toronto, which is the main point for your consideration. So much for a poor young country like Canada building a railway in the most thriftless and extravagant manner, alongside an unrivalled natural water communication.

Only *one-tenth* of the wheat and flour of Upper Canada were marketed in Montreal last year, which is a startling fact. They won't buy our fall wheat. It has all to be sold to Americans, and the G. T. R. carries no fall wheat except the portion shipped for consumption in Maine and Boston. The whole of our fall wheat, and the greater portion of our fall wheat flour, and all our barley, have to be shipped across lake Ontario, as our best markets for these articles are along the Erie canal, in the rich towns accessible therefrom, and in the great city of New York. Buffalo also receives for distribution a small portion of our produce, when western stuff is deficient in quality or quantity. Lower Canada and those fishing villages on the Atlantic coast will never be to us the markets that the commercial and manufacturing centres of the United States are and have been; the very possibility is forbidden by their poverty and geographical position.

Therefore you should so endeavour to arrange the arteries of your trade that they may lead direct to those markets where your products are most appreciated, and where, in consequence, the highest prices can be realized for them.

The following extracts from the Honble. T. F. Hatch's Report on Internal Commerce and Transportation, to the United States Government, contain sound teaching on these and kindred subjects, which are worthy of your careful attention.

Mr. Hatch says:—" In the New World the chief effort of

statesmanship, applied to material objects, is to develop as early and to as great an extent as is possible the resources of our own territories. Other nations are compelled to seek abroad for those means of employment and prosperity which we possess at home, and to an extent practically unlimited. This development is the chief object of our wisest political economy; and it can in no other way be so well promoted as by constructing or enlarging the various means of communication which carry emigrants to those regions where their toil will be most amply rewarded, and at the same time bring the productions of all parts of our common country to those markets where they command the highest price, or, in other words, return the greatest remuneration to human labour. We thus also stimulate immigration from abroad, and provide the essential elements for the most profitable foreign trade.

"Commerce has always in every country sought the first channels formed by nature, as the easiest and cheapest highways from the interior to the seaboard.

"Hitherto, in the gigantic struggles for the internal carrying trade of our own country, railways have not been successful competitors with our inland routes of communication by water, for the carriage of heavy or bulky articles during the seasons of navigation. The question is determined by the different results of motive power applied to land and water. An elaborate investigation shows the following results, as exemplified by a fair comparison of the relative cost of transportation by rail, and the other means of conveyance best known in the United States;

	Excess of cost per cent. greater.
By rail over ocean transportation	733.3
By rail over great lakes	525.0
By rail over Mississippi and St. Lawrence Transportation	316.6
By rail over Hudson	400.0
By rail over Illinois improvement	257.1
By rail over Erie canal enlarged	215.0
By rail over ordinary canal	150.0

"Boats or vessels, if made of wood, and propelled either by sail or steam-engine, will endure for many years. If made of iron, which, before many years have elapsed, will probably supersede wood as the chief material for ship-building, they will last a century. They run through water which costs nothing, and does not wear out. A crew of five or six men can manage a canal steamer of 600 tons, and ten or twenty men are sufficient for a lake ship or steamer of 600 or 1,200 tons. On the other hand, a railway and its trains of cars, each of which can carry only 150 or 200 tons of freight, are subject to great loss from ordinary and necessary wear and tear need continual replacement and repairs, require a much larger proportion of men to watch and manage them, and are rapidly worn out by a stress of increased business, which, comparatively, would do little injury to a canal.

"It is stated, as curiously illustrative of the comparative cheapness of carriage by rail and the ocean, that a ship recently arrived at Philadelphia from San Francisco, having brought a cargo of wheat at nearly the same freight it would have cost from Chicago to Philadelphia by rail.

"For the reasons thus elucidated, the freight on railways, where they enter into competition with the ordinary means of water communication, consists for a considerable proportion of the year chiefly of the lighter and more costly articles requiring rapid transit and delivery, while ordinary products of the West, in quantities so great that it is difficult to form an adequate understanding of their magnitude, are carried on our lakes, rivers and canals. With the increase of Western cultivation and production thus occasioned by the cheapest possible freight during the milder months, the amount of railroad travel is also multiplied, as well as the consumption of those articles for which carriage by rail is eagerly sought at advanced rates.

"It thus becomes evident that in attempting to find a solution of our chief commercial problems, and estimating the comparative importance of the various routes to the ocean from the West, duly examining the physical characteristics of the country, and the natural adaptation of its different sections to internal commerce, and the cheap delivery of freight, the great saving effected by the use of water communication must be borne in mind.

"The remarkable increase thus exemplified in the progress of the West is chiefly due to the construction of the railroads, to which the surface of their country is so well adapted, bringing produce to the great lakes, over which, and by the connecting links of eastern canals and rivers, it reaches our seaports.

"In 1850 these States had only 1,263 miles of railroad; fourteen years later, in 1864, they had 12,519 miles in operation, and no less than 18,136 either completed or in progress of construction.

"A distinguished United States Senator from the north-west explained the methods by which, in Wisconsin, Minnesota, and Iowa, certain railroad companies had become so far consolidated as to constitute almost a complete monopoly for transportation in those States, with the natural result of exorbitant freights, unjustly putting money into the pockets of the few at the expense of the producers of national wealth. The Senator, on behalf of the people of his country, protested against regarding the Erie canal 'in any other light than as a national work,' stating in strong terms his reluctance 'to let a company occupy the only unoccupied ground for a transit route that there is between the Mississippi river and the Atlantic ocean, and then set all people that are west of it at defiance, and charge just such tolls as they choose.'

"The Board of Trade of St. Paul reported, July 5, 1865, that 'freight on grain from St. Paul and other river towns north of Winona to Chicago is now thirty cents per bushel, and has most of the time for the last two years exceeded that figure.' Even now it is stated that the farmers of Minnesota are paying forty cents freight upon a bushel of wheat to Chicago or Milwaukee. This is a higher freight than the western shipper has paid during the last year upon grain from Chicago to our seaport cities *via* the lakes and New York canals, the average freight of the season being much lower. Accusations against eastern lines of transportation for exorbitant prices certainly proceed with an ill grace from States where the farmer cannot move the product of his labour out of his own State without paying charges more than sufficient to eat it up."

EXTRACT FROM A SPEECH OF SENATOR BENNETT.

"New Orleans, I see from the exchanges of that city, is making Herculean efforts to draw the trade of the West down the Mississippi. Heretofore they have had no elevators there for handling grain. They are moving to secure the advantage that elevators give. I understand Western parties are going there with capital, to give New Orleans the great benefit of large elevators. It will be remembered there are no tolls on the Mississippi river. The distance is greater, but that is of small account as compared with water routes unrestricted by tolls. They are bringing into operation on the Mississippi transportation by barges, towed by tugs, one tug taking a large number of barges in tow, the same as on the Hudson river. There were tows that went down the Mississippi from the upper portion of that river last season with between one and two hundred thousand bushels of grain in one large tow. The Chambers of Commerce of St. Louis and New Orleans have this question of barge transportation under discussion, and are determined to draw the business of the West by what they call the great natural channel to the city of New Orleans. St. Louis and New Orleans are working together with might and main for the accomplishment of the before-mentioned object —to draw the trade of the great West to the Gulf of Mexico. The superiority of free water transportation is shown by a recent event. The ship *David Crocket*, during December last, arrived at Philadelphia in ninety-four days from San Francisco, with a cargo of seventy-six thousand bushels of wheat, subject to a freight of only fifty-eight cents per bushel of sixty pounds. The distance is about eighteen thousand miles.

"The railroad rate this winter on wheat, from Chicago to Philadelphia, is 51 cents per bushel of 60 pounds, and the distance is only eight hundred and twenty-four miles."

These are the views of distinguished gentlemen who are the able advocates of immense interests, to which our " Little Central Railway" bears no more comparison than does a contract for opening up a new concession road to the gigantic operations of Jackson, Peto, Brassy and Betts; and having considered them attentively, you will see the folly of delivering yourselves over, all well and securely bound, into the hands of the G. T. R. Company, who will take very good care that henceforward you will be free from the risks of the "dangers of navigation," and be effectually cut out from the cheapest highway to the best markets, by the route to Toronto and the waterways.

Add to these facts the knowledge that the G. T. R. has been, and will continue to be, unable to move with reasonable dispatch over *its whole length* the produce of U. C., especially the coarser kinds of freights, obtained from the woods, and does not and will not, as long as it can be avoided, carry freight to this port, and you have incontrovertible reasons why you should not encourage the thriftless idea, lately advanced by one of your representatives, of building a railway from your county to Stratford or Seaforth, to act as a feeder to an anaconda, of such slow, but expensive digestion, as the G. T. R.

Million after million has been tossed, under various pretexts, into its voracious maw, and yet it continues hungry.

Our Local Parliament will have no more important duty to consider than how to encourage the construction and extension of the means of communication, which will *carry out the trees and carry in the people* to those places where their toil will reward their employers, and provide themselves with means, in a few years, to employ those whom they will invite by their prosperity to leave the old "sod" and join them, in prosperous Canada.

Our immigration business drags, somehow. Of the few who come determined to settle in Canada, a portion re-emigrate to the States; mainly because they cannot afford to buy dear wild land, and are afraid to "tackle the trees," burn them, and have to wait two years before they can eat bread of their own growing. The construction of cheap railways, bound by law to carry cordwood, would in many instances remove those difficulties; therefore these roads ought to be built, and pushed into the heart of the country, and people *brought* to form the nucleus of settlements, wherever settlements were possible.

If the British Government would place at the disposal of our Confederate Government a half dozen of the old wooden men-of-war, with men enough to work them, and if our own Government would furnish the provisions, and send to an English, Irish, Scotch, or German port, one ship each, to secure at Whitsuntide the farm labourers, bring them here free, and give each head of a family, or young man, a ticket securing him one or two years' employment with a farmer, or other person, according to a pre-arranged plan, and a location ticket for 100 acres of land, to be patented on the fulfilment of certain defined conditions, *we would have plenty of immigrants.*

The class referred to is poor, and cannot move without

assistance. The same course could be pursued among the poor miners of Norway and Sweden, who would be the most desirable immigrants for the extensive mineral and agricultural region round the Georgian Bay and eastwards. If a free passage both ways were offered men from the section of country to which the "man-of-peace" was bound, each voyage, spring and fall, and some advertising judiciously done, they would soon obtain the desired complement of immigrants. Men who immigrated to this country, and arrived poor, but who by their economy and industry have got comparatively rich as farmers, are the right sort of emigration agents to send on these missions. Each farmer or other party requiring hired assistance could send their ticket to the captain for the sort of help required, and the law could be made to make the contract binding on both sides. A great portion of the expense could be recovered by charging the immigrant one or two months' wages, payable on arrival, by the farmer, or by the immigrant after the expiry of one year. These vessels could carry home deals, &c., and make a great deal more, perhaps, than the expense of the voyage. By this means thousands of steady and laborious poor people would suddenly find themselves on the road to an unexpected independence.

It is unnecessary to enlarge on the general increase of material wealth to be derived by your counties and this city from the construction of a sufficient railway, on a basis of sound engineering and commercial principles, to connect your counties, and the large fertile intervening tract of country, with this city, and through it, with all the rich and important cities of New York and neighbouring States, containing a population of twelve millions of people, who are our natural and indispensable customers for our choicest productions, and who will continue to be so, notwithstanding their present erratic legislation.

You will clearly see how your interests *are to be advanced* by stations becoming market towns, and how idle water privileges will become, under the stimulus of railway traffic, busy centres of manufacturing industry. Household comforts, now beyond the reach of many, will be easily attainable in exchange for all your minor farm produce, wood, &c. All this, you say, is apparent, but you do not see your way to getting the railroad.

There is a difficulty in getting a railroad, because the waste, extravagance and mismanagement attending the construction of our present lines have rendered them unprofitable. The money spent in their construction, so far as the first shareholders are concerned, has been *totally lost*, excepting in the case of the Great Western Railway. The system of paying contractors their own exorbitant prices, if they took stock in part payment, was ruinous. In consequence of this untoward state of matters, not a dollar can be borrowed to construct much needed lines on the most thoroughly economical principles, without some more tangible basis than mere Canada Railroad Stocks.

It is contrary to the genius of our Government to guarantee the interest on outlays for purely local works; therefore, sufficient land must be obtained from the Local Government to induce capitalists, or men with any spare means in Canada and elsewhere, to take the requisite amount of stock in these roads to secure their immediate construction.

If every $100 stock carried with it a patent or scrip for a *certain lot* of 100 acres of land, and if these bonds and the land scrip were saleable and transferable, separately or together, the amount of money required to build a cheap, light, Narrow-Gauge Railway, on the Central Route, would very quickly be forthcoming, and the scream of the locomotive would very soon awaken the echoes of your solitudes, and startle your population into sudden activity and prosperity; and *yourselves* would largely benefit from the credit derived from land, which, under present circumstances, not one in one thousand of our people of the present generation will ever see. Of course I refer to the land east of the Georgian Bay, north of the new townships, all the way to and beyond lake Nipissing, to which the people of Toronto propose in time to extend the line projected to Gull River.

Who are so well entitled to the use of the Crown Lands, as a basis of credit for promoting important and necessary public works, as the very men by whose hardships, toil and industry these lands have been rendered or are likely to be made of any practical value, and who are the parties mainly to be benefited by the construction of these railroads?

It would be highly impolitic, in view of the progress desired for the country, as well as cruel to these less favoured settlers, to deny them the advantages obtained at such enormous and unnecessary cost, by those who live in more favoured localities.

The land will not be *removed*, and these roads, for which a small portion of it is sold, will be the very means of filling it with immigrants.

The Government sold last year, in the County of Simcoe, 30,000 or 40,000 acres of land, at public auction at Barrie, at prices varying from 10c. to 20c. an acre; what, therefore, is the worth of the unbroken wilderness round lake Nipissing?—*Not a farthing*, unless we point a railroad in that direction, *which cannot be done* without direct assistance from the Government, or by the aid of a land grant. The Grand Trunk style of railroad, and cost, is beyond our power under any circumstances. Therefore we must *go canny*, and seek the establishment of a system of railways more suitable to our means and requirements, as has been successfully done in Australia, India, Norway and Sweden.

As much as possible of the stocks of these two new railways, one to run north-west and the other north-east of this city, should be taken by the people of the country traversed and the people of Toronto, so as to secure local management and proper attention to local interests.

The following extracts from a pamphlet by J. Edward Boyd, Civil Engineer, New Brunswick, and extracts from the report of Mr. Fitzgibbon, Chief Engineer to the Government of Queensland, Australia, will explain more authoritatively and clearly to you the nature of the cheap light narrow gauge system, from which you will infer its suitableness for local routes in Canada.

Mr. Boyd says :—" The cost of a railway is, all other conditions being similar, controlled to a great extent by the gauge. Assuming a gauge of 5 feet 6 inches for Trunk lines, it by no means follows that for tributary lines and independent lines in country districts, a narrow gauge (say 3 feet) might not be introduced with advantage. It is conceded that the resistance due to curves decreases as the width between the rails is reduced, as sharper curves could therefore be introduced without a corresponding increase in the resistance.

"Heavy earthworks could be avoided, without resort to steep gradients, and narrow gauge tributaries could be carried into many districts when lines of the wider gauge would be enormously expensive, in both construction and operation.

"This reduction of the gauge would be followed by a diminution of the cost of every part of the road, from the *turning of the first sod to the driving of the last spike,* as follows :—Saving on earth, 50 per cent.; on masonry, 25 per cent.; the engines would weigh from twelve to fourteen tons, instead of twenty-eight tons; and the weight of the rails, chairs, &c., being proportionately less, the cost of permanent way *would be about one-half,* with a corresponding reduction in the cost of rolling stock.

"The railway of narrowest gauge used for passenger traffic, worked by locomotives, is in Merionetshire, Wales—gauge, 2 feet. Between June, 1863, and February, 1865, the four engines employed on this road (7½ tons) had run 57,000 miles without leaving the rails—the steepest gradient being 1 in 60. Up these gradients, these engines take a load of 50 tons at ten miles an hour; sharpest curves on the line, 132 feet radius.

"In the colliery districts of England and Wales there are lines of 2 feet 4 inches, 2 feet 6 inches, and 2 feet 8 inches, which are used with great success.

"The Norwegian lines have a gauge of 3 feet 6 inches; engines weigh 14 tons; speed 15 miles an hour. A gauge of 3 feet 9 inches has been successfuly worked in Belguim. Upon a line three feet gauge, passenger trains could be run at 15 to 20 miles an hour, the carriages being say 7 feet 6 inches wide inside—ample room for comfortable seats—less width would answer freight cars."

Mr. Boyd quotes as follows from Mr. Fitzgibbon, Chief Engineer to the Government of Queensland, Australia:—

"A railway of 3 feet 6 inches gauge will accommodate a traffic of 400 tons of goods and 800 passengers in each twelve hours. During the nine months ending 30th September, 1866, the average daily traffic on the E. and N. A. Railway was 484 passengers and 185 tons freight, and on the N. S. Railway, 400 passengers and 180 tons freight.

"On 22 miles of one line, when it passes over the Little Liverpool and Main Ranges, numerous curves of 5 chains radius are introduced, in order to avoid the heavy works in excavation, tunnelling, viaducts, &c., which the use of curves of a larger radius would involve; but had a gauge of 4 feet 8½ inches been adopted, curves of 8 chains radius (as used in crossing the Blue Mountains in New South Wales) would have been necessary; and it was found, on a calculation of the quantities of work, that the cost of the line with 4 feet 8½ inch gauge would exceed that of the 3 feet 6 inch gauge by more than three-fold.

"Taking the item of permanent way, we find that on the New South Wales lines the cost per mile is £2,996 7s. 6d.; while on one 3 feet 6 inch gauge line the cost is £2,162 4s. 0d. per mile, including broken stone ballast; giving a difference of £834 per mile in favour of the narrow gauge.

"A statement which is appended to the report shows that, taking an equal quantity of rolling stock on each line, the cost of that of the 3 feet 6 inch gauge is 64⅓ per cent. of the cost on the 4 feet 6 inch gauge.

"It appears that a speed of over 20 miles an hour has been attained on the 3 feet 6 inch line, without any perceptible oscillation or unsteadiness of the carriages, which are roomy and comfortable, and give the greatest satisfaction to the public.

"*Mr. Fitzgibbon maintains that it is the wisest possible policy to provide only for the wants we now foresee, and to carry out effectually a system of railways which is within our present means, leaving posterity to decide what further expenditure should be incurred to meet its wants.*

"Again, to expend two or three times the necessary amount now, with a view to meeting a want which cannot be felt for perhaps twenty years or more, is simply to expend in interest alone a sum sufficient to re-build an entirely new system of communication.

"The construction of the road, and the various appliances employed, are in all respects equal to any railway in the world, excepting only that they are limited in power to the wants of the case."

Mr. Boyd contends that if the diminution of cost is so great as between a 3 feet 6 inch gauge and one of 4 feet 8 inches, the difference between one of 3 feet and of 5 feet 6 inches is certainly not estimated at 50 per cent.

The same author remarks, in a subsequent letter, that "after fully discussing the matter, the Swedish engineers have decided upon a 3 feet 6 inch gauge for all local lines or feeders—and several of such having been built during the last few years, are giving entire satisfaction. In one of those the embankments are 13 feet broad; weight of rails, 37 lbs. per yard, connected with fish plates, speed, 16 miles an hour, but occasionally brought up to 30 and 35 miles an hour."

The following extract from "Engineering," published in London, England, explains itself, and is convincing proof of the adaptability of the 3 ft. 6 in. gauge to our Central Road, and many other routes in Canada.

The paragraph in italics was not italicised in the original. It accords exactly with the views so clearly set forth by Mr. Fitzgibbon, from the antipodes of Norway. Wherever expressed, these truths are as irresistible as Palliser's spherical chilled shot.

"THE 3-FEET 6-INCH RAILWAY GAUGE.

"TO THE EDITOR OF 'ENGINEERING.'

"SIR,—By request of my friend Mr. C. Pihl, chief engineer of the Norwegian Government railways, I beg to hand you the enclosed paper on the 3 ft. 6 in. railway gauge, and knowing well the trustworthiness of his practical experience, I have no doubt that by inserting it in your valuable periodical much additional light would be thrown on the question to which it relates.

"I remain, Sir, your obedient Servant,
"W. TOTTIE,
"Royal Swedish and Norwegian Consulate-General,
"London, March 7, 1867."

CHEAP RAILWAYS.

"SIR,—In 'ENGINEERING,' of 4th January, I find, in an article headed 'Railways in Lilliput,' views with regard to the 3 ft. 6 in. gauge railway system (as carried out in Queensland, India, and Norway), which are so much at variance with the experience gained in this country, where railways of this description have been in full operation since 1861, that you will allow me, no doubt, as the engineer of the lines, to make a few remarks, which may possibly be acceptable to those of your readers who feel interested in this matter.

"In your article you ask what is to compensate for the manifest disadvantages of the 3 ft. 6 in. gauge, and for an answer refer to a letter which Mr. Wm. T. Doyne, Memb. Inst. C.E., has lately published in Queensland, in which he says he considers that the safe maximum speed on the 3 ft. 6 in. gauge cannot exceed ten or, at most, twelve miles an hour, and that, although he has travelled twenty-two miles an hour on this gauge, he doubts whether the working stock would admit of it, except in the case of the engine running down steep gradients; and he states that he would feel more at his ease on a line of ordinary gauge at fifty miles an hour. He further says: 'In Queensland the features of the country 'enforce the use of five-chain curves, and consequently a 3 'ft. 6 in. gauge.' On this you make the following remarks: 'Before engineers inflict a wholly insufficient gauge upon the 'railway system of a colony, they should first ascertain 'whether, even with curves of minimum radii, rolling stock 'cannot be constructed to work them upon the ordinary 'gauge;' and, in concluding your article, you say that the same remarks apply to India and Norway.

"With regard to the information received from, and opinions formed on the Queensland Railway, it is not for me to make any remark, except when they affect the system, and are at variance with facts gained by experience. My intentions are not, however, to enter into any polemical discussion, as the 4 ft. 8½ in. as well as the 3 ft. 6 in. gauge systems have been in operation here for many years. There is no doubt or uncertainty with us about the question at issue; and I will, therefore, merely give facts and results as supplementary to the information you are already in possession of from Queensland, and which may be of interest to those who wish to investigate the subject.

"When it is said that the adoption of the narrow gauge has been enforced by the necessity for sharp curves, the conjecture is not quite in accordance with the facts of the case here, as we have hitherto been able to avoid curves of less than 11 chains. *With us it has been a question of providing a railway communication at a comparatively small cost in a country of large extent, with little traffic and limited resources; and although the greater facility of traversing sharp curves is a decided and no unimportant advantage to be gained by the use of the small gauge, this consideration has not enforced its adoption here. It has been in this case the choice between a cheap and efficient railway or none.*

"With what success these lines have been carried out we shall see. I will now give the cost of three separate railways, which I built at the same time, under equal circumstances, and with the same view as to economy and efficiency; the one line, the Kongsvinger line, of 4 ft. 8½ in. gauge, with a length of fifty-six miles, has cost £6,350 per mile, including stations and rolling stock, but no workshops; the Hamar-Elverum line, of 3 ft. 6 in. gauge, and twenty-four miles only, has cost £3,142 per mile, including stations, rolling stock, and small workshops; the third line, the Throndjem-Stören Railway, also of 3 ft. 6 in. gauge, and thirty-one and a half miles long, has cost £5,300, including everything. At the present time there are fifty-six miles more (the Dramman-Randsfjord Railway, of the same narrow gauge) under construction, the half of which is temporarily opened for traffic. This line is calculated at £4,563 per mile, and for this sum I have no doubt it will be completed. On the two last-named lines the works are comparatively very heavy; the country which we have had to go through has been difficult to deal with, and necessitated many extensive works, such as cuttings (to a great extent in hard rock), frequent bridges and viaducts, some of timber and some of iron, several exceeding 70 ft in height and of considerable length. Besides these, there are extensive and comparatively costly stone works along the declivities by the side of the rivers and hills.

"The regular trains are run here at 14 miles an hour, including stoppages, or 16 to 20 miles between stations, the very same speed at which the mixed trains run on the 4 ft. 8½ in. gauge here. As to the safety of fast running, engines and carriages appear to run as safely and steadily at 30 miles an hour on the 3 ft. 6 in. gauge as they do on one of 4 ft. 8½ in., and I have run the very engine illustrated in your journal of 21st December last at upwards of 40 miles an hour, with as much feeling of ease and security as I have felt when running any engine on a broader gauge. The engines, as well as the rest of the rolling stock, are constructed with an angle of stability fully as great as in rolling stock for an ordinary gauge; this, with a sufficient minimum load on the axle, being the principal condition for stability, leaves the gauge as a factor of practically small importance in limiting the speed. The working stock, when substantially and judiciously constructed, is as durable in one case as in the other. In stating these facts it is not my intention to advocate as high a speed on these lines, with light engines of only 3 ft. to 3 ft. 9 in. driving wheels, as on lines of a broader gauge; they are not designed for high speed, but to suit circumstances where this is of a secondary consideration.

"When the difficulties in the construction of an efficient rolling stock for this gauge have been satisfactorily overcome, the one gauge being as empirical as the other, it then becomes in my opinion the duty of the engineer to decide which gauge is best adapted to the requirements of the country. If the 4 ft. 8½ in. gauge is sufficient for a country with vast traffic and ample resources, the 3 ft. 6 in. gauge may be all that is required in places less favourably situated. Should, however, that fortunate time arrive (say in the course of fifteen or twenty years), when the traffic has developed itself to such an extent that the line, as originally constructed, proves insufficient, then I believe that a double line would naturally suggest itself as meeting the requirements of increased traffic in every way better than a single line of wider gauge. The cost of the addition would, based upon calculations made for this purpose, be rather more than 50 per cent. (without much variation) of the original cost of the line proper, stations and rolling stock not included, and the total of this double line would then cost about the same as the single 4 ft. 8½ in. would originally have cost. I can, therefore, not see the necessity or justice of having the gauge wider to suit increasing demands in the one case rather than in the other, as long as there is the same facility of adding proportionally to the working power. There is certainly a greater difference in the producing capabilities or the traffic of the various countries than there is here in the gauges. What may befit one country, is therefore not in place in another, and it therefore is neccessary here, as elsewhere, to adapt the means to the end. The amount of interest on the difference in the original outlay between the two lines would consequently have been lost during the assumed period, besides the excess of expense of keeping up the wider line.

"In proof of the slight difference in the cost of the two systems, there has been adduced the amount of earthwork in a bank 50 ft. high, the formation width of which has been set down at 14 ft. in one case and 12 ft. in the other. This I cannot consider fair. The formation width for the line of 4 ft. 8½ in. guage is generally from 15 ft. to 18 ft., say 16½ ft. on an average (it is here 18 ft.), and for the 3 ft. 6 in. gauge it is here 12 ft. 6 in. (The reason why the latter is reduced so much, I suppose, is obvious). The average height of the banks and cuttings on the narrower gauge is less than on the broad, owing to the greater facility of adaptation to the country. With us the height is 10 ft., whereas, had the broader gauge been adopted, it would have been 12 ft. to 14 ft., say 13 ft. This would make, with the same slope as in your example, the proportion as 225 to 383 1-7, or nearly as 4 to 7, instead of 31 to 32, as stated. You have, however, used the slope 1 to 1, which would make my figures less favourable than the above.

"I find that I have already gone more at length into this discussion than was my intention, and am prepared for doubts being entertained as to the correctness of the conclusions which I arrived at from the facts here set forth.

"Of many to whom the subject may be of real importance, few will probably be able personally to study the subject on the spot in India and Queensland; but with the present easy communication between England and this country, any one willing to devote nine or ten days to the purpose may conveniently see and judge for himself; and I can assure all such visitors that they will meet with every facility for obtaining all the information they may desire.

"I am, Sir,
"Yours respectfully,
"C. PIHL.

"Christiana, February 25, 1867."

The following extracts from a letter received by the writer from the eminent English engineering firm, Sir Charles Fox & Son, bearing directly on the question in hand, will be read with much interest, and will command the attention due to the statements and opinions of gentlemen of such world-wide experience and high standing :—

"We have been requested by Mr. Middleton to communicate with you upon the subject of Light Railways, which we have much pleasure in doing, as this is a matter to which we have given much attention.

"We are the Consulting Engineers to the Colonial Government of Queensland, which is now engaged in constructing upwards of 200 miles of railway of 3 ft. 6 in.—of which 50 miles have been for some time open for traffic—and has also under survey some 200 miles more. These lines are for the most part made through an undeveloped country, for the purpose of opening it up, and for a portion of their length pass through very mountainous districts, involving heavy works.

"The principle adopted on these lines is to make them in the very best manner, to spare no necessary expense to ensure materials and workmanship of first-class quality, but so to adapt them in every way to the traffic to be expected, without the evil generally accompanying such economy, of heavy working and maintenance expenses. These lines are suitable for Passenger and Goods traffic with trains weighing 150 tons gross, exclusive of the locomotives, travelling at an average speed, including stoppages, of 20 miles per hour. They are laid with iron rails weighing 40 lbs. to the yard, flat-bottomed, properly fished at the joints, and secured with fang-bolts and dog-spikes to transverse rectangular hard-wood sleepers 2' 6" to 3' 0" apart from centre to centre. The bridges, which are very numerous and heavy for the most part, have lattice girders of wrought iron. The chief stations are also of wrought iron lined with wood, and have been sent out complete from this country. The rolling stock is of the very best description, and the passenger carriages quite equal for comfort to the best in this country. The locomotives weigh from 15 to 16 tons when ready for the road, and are capable of travelling with ease at the working speed and with the load before referred to, on ruling gradients of 1 in 100, with curves of 330 ft. radius. By the use, however, of locomotives of a slightly heavier class, gradients of 1 in 40 can be worked with ease with similar curves.

"The ruling principle throughout is, that no wheel shall, under any circumstances, have more than 3 tons upon it, and that the speed shall not exceed a maximum of 30 miles per hour, and every detail is adapted to these data.

"We have also, in conjunction with another Engineer, constructed a line in India upon the 3′ 6″ guage, as a tributary to the Madras Railway. This line passes through an easy country, excepting that there were a good many bridges, in order to provide waterway. The land was provided by the Government, and the works were carried out by the Company's own Engineer. The rails weigh 36 lbs. to the yard, laid on transverse teak sleepers. The rolling stock and engines are only so far different from those used in Queensland as is necessary to meet the difference of climate. The stations are large bungalows, with ample accommodation. The line is single, with passing places. *The total cost of the works, including freight from England, management, &c., has been only £3,200 per mile, or, including rolling stock, stations and stores, £3,800 per mile. The line has now been worked for some time most satisfactorily, the trains having on several occasions attained a speed of 40 miles an hour, and the working expenses being moderate.*

"Similar lines are at work in Norway with most satisfactory results, the cost varying, according to the character of the country, from £3,000 to £6,000 per mile, including everything."

The success of these sort of Railways is not problematical, it is an ascertained fact, proven by years of experience. Our Railroad managers, through their engineers and otherwise, may attack the system proposed on the Central Route, by a new company, as a means of defeating the building *of any railway* on this route, but with your active and energetic co-operation, the "little road" will be built, as it is favored and promoted by the most wealthy and influential citizens of Toronto, who lack neither skill, means nor energy, to secure for yourselves and the citizens of Toronto the benefits of *a direct road bound to carry cordwood* from your vast counties. Mr. Fowler's scheme did not interest the citizens of Toronto, because they *knew* the money for such a road could not be obtained, and he was easily overpowered by Mr. Cumberland's Northern Railway friends and the apathy of the supporters of the Central Route, although *numbering all other citizens* excepting those who were afraid the Central Route might connect with the G. T. R. at a point west of this city. The parties now interested have no such fears ; nor have they any view to big contracts, for their personal gain, which may have influenced public opinion as to Mr. Fowler's programme, as well as that of the promoters of the Durham Branch. The adoption of a system of small contracts, in building new roads, is *sure* protection from the depredations of large contractors, who despise such two-penny half-penny ways of doing business.

Contracts, so small as to be within the reach of local contractors, are the essence of cheap railway making.

The merchants of Toronto, the nature of whose business teaches them to understand the routes of traffic best calculated to promote the prosperity of the country, are thoroughly alive to the necessity of preventing the very sources of their trade from being dried up by the formation of lines of railroad to connect with second-rate markets, objectionable and expensive harbours, or with railroads the policy of which is inimical to the true interests of the country and of this city.

You may depend upon it, no effort will be spared to secure for this city her just share of the trade of the interior, and the benefit of being the terminus for two such promising lines of railroad, either of which will bring more farm or forest produce to this market than any of the other three. Along the routes of the new lines our merchants would find their business increase three or five-fold. Our workshops, warehouses and vessels would be taxed to the limits of their capacity, in supplying facilities for the new business which these roads would pour into the city. Property would increase in value, not by reason of undue speculation, but on account of the competition for premises to accomodate an increasing and busy population. Taxes would be lightened in proportion as the number and means increased of those from whom they were to be collected.

Not one dollar is wanted from the city, in its corporate capacity, to assist in the construction of the cheap railways;

a large amount, however, will be subscribed by the merchants and property-holders individually, and the city is expected to give, free from rent or taxes, right of way, access to the harbour, and room for the premises of the Railway Companies; privileges, to purchase which, you will understand, would *cost a great deal of money*.

It is important to remember, in consulting amongst yourselves what railroad policy it is your interest to support, that in addition to its unrivalled commercial and shipping advantages, *Toronto is now* the seat of our Local Government, as well as the legal, financial, commercial, educational and industrial capital of Ontario. *Any other* terminus of your railways must be at comparatively small places with indifferent markets.

A worse fate, for your interests, would result from terminating your railways *on other roads*, which would exact, as usual, heavy toll for their share in the carriage of your stuff to the water and the leading markets. I need not repeat that the lowest freight by the most direct line, to the best market and shipping point, should be your governing motive in selecting routes for your traffic.

An independent line to the water, worked, not in the interest of the Great Western Railway, Grand Trunk Railway, or Northern Railway, but in the interest of your Counties and Toronto, is the only line worthy of your consideration.

A line to Guelph is only a little less objectionable than one to Stratford—either is not possible under existing charters. The capital will not be forthcoming for such unnecessarily expensive roads. Toronto has the power and the influence to build a road on the central route to Durham, thence, *via* Walkerton, to a point on Lake Huron, with a branch from Durham to Owen Sound, and, with or without encouragement, will set about the construction of the road as soon as practicable.

In the appendix you will find the names of the Provisional Officers of the Company who have undertaken this good work, and who are a guarantee that it will be well and truly performed. Leave nothing undone which may assist them. You must not wait until *somebody builds you a road;* you must be up and doing; a great deal depends on yourselves.

Less money than you once offered is enough to secure you the Central Road—only you must give it *active support.*

Communications or suggestions anent the business of the Toronto, Bruce & Grey Railway Company, addressed to their Secretary, Mr. WILLIAM S. TAYLOR, Toronto, will receive prompt attention.

I am, gentlemen,
Your obedient servant,
G. LAIDLAW.

APPENDIX.

To the Wardens of North Ontario and Victoria,
and the People on the Route of the Toronto and Nippissing Railway.

GENTLEMEN,—

Being desirous of submitting to your consideration the views and statements expressed in the preceding pages, *in so far as they are applicable to your case,* without entailing the loss of time and expense involved in preparing a mere repetition for a separate publication, I have added a letter written by myself, in reply to a communication, in the "Leader" newspaper, from Lindsay, and a few other remarks which, I trust, may be of service in calling your attention and arousing your energies to take active measures to co-operate with the Toronto & Nipissing Railway Company, just formed in this city, to secure for you the advantages of a Railway, and, for Toronto, a large accession of new business, without taking it from any other place. The "Leader's" anonymous correspondent stated that the Lindsay & Port Hope Railway is capable of doing the business of the country for the next thirty years. Nonsense! In thirty years there will be larger towns thirty, aye, sixty miles further north than Lindsay. The Toronto & Nipissing Railway will create those towns. Lindsay meanwhile will prosper with the general prosperity of the surrounding townships.

There is not an acre of land in North Ontario or Victoria, nor a bushel of grain, nor a saw-log, nor an horse nor cow, sheep nor lamb, neither pigs nor poultry, neither cord of wood nor pack of wool, which would not be greatly increased in value by the competition engendered, and by the facilities afforded by a railway to this superior metropolitan market. Put your shoulders to the wheel, and very soon you will have markets at your doors for every article of farm produce and every stick in your woods.

Reading and gossiping about the new railway won't build it. You must take active and decisive steps at once to encourage and assist the gentlemen who have undertaken the onerous task of constructing this line of railway.

"Suas è a Claun-nan-Gael."

I commend to your careful attention the annexed list of the Provisional Officers elected by the Toronto and Nipissing Railway Company, whose very names are a warrant to you for immediate activity and success.

Your obedient servant,
G. LAIDLAW.

"CHEAP RAILWAYS.

"To the Editor of the 'Leader.'

"Sir,—From the tenor of your anonymous Lindsay correspondent's letter, he is liable to the suspicion of being a Georgian Bay Canal dreamer, who may have borrowed spectacles from Lindsay with which to examine one of the cheap railway schemes, with a view to a flank attack through them on the opponents of the canal.

"In replying to 'Observer's' irresponsible statements, I presume, Mr. Editor, that you would not open your columns to any local writer who aimed maliciously to mar the construction of a very desirable, practicable and promising public work, calculated to increase the area, the value of the land and its products, and the population of the territory to the north-east of us, the trade of which is naturally tributary to Toronto.

"The Toronto and Nipissing Railway was not projected to oppose the Port Hope and Lindsay Railroad, or rob either it or these towns of any of their well-earned business.

"The proposed route of the new road will pass about fifteen miles north of Lindsay, the northern terminus of the P. N. and L. R. The latter runs south-east, the former south-west, which renders competition along their routes impossible.

"But, while we do not want to rob them of the handling of a board or a spar, we will have the share that the capital and enterprise of this city may secure for itself of the produce of the interminable forests that stretch northwards, beyond the immediate vicinity of Lindsay 200 miles to Lake Nipissing. The immediate settlement and weal and prosperity of the people already settled in great numbers in the nearer portions of that immense country, (and whose lumbering and mercantile interests are mainly sustained by the banking institutions and wholesale merchants of this city,) are general public benefits, which will follow the sagacious extension or multiplication of the means of communication between this city and the interior, and which will benefit Lindsay not less than Toronto. A sudden and rapid increase in the value of land, pine, farm produce, and the opening up of mines, would create such prosperity as would redound to the advantage of every man in Lindsay, and in the townships to the northward.

"I am not aware of a single mine having been opened, or even discovered, on the route of our railway; but those who know the 'geography below the ground,' say there are big indications! and if our capitalists saw them, and a road for their products to market, they might be induced to sink some shafts. The nature and the cost of the road will be explained on better authority than mine in a fortnight.

"The route proposed will traverse for the first 75 miles one of the finest districts in Upper Canada, rich in agricultural resources, and well settled; one end of it will be carried well into the pine forests, while the other will terminate at the best harbour on the north shore of Lake Ontario, from whence freights are cheaper than from any other north shore port, because the largest vessels can here load, get return cargoes, and seek a safe shelter. It is said the exports from Port Hope last season were 65,000,000 feet of lumber, or nearly 500 cargoes of 130,000 feet each. This large trade accounts for the purchase by Port Hope merchants, from Toronto owners, of a great many schooners, which used to be the pride of our harbour.

"The Northern Railroad is reported to have carried and shipped last year 41,000,000 feet of lumber, only two-thirds of the exports of Port Hope.

"Your correspondent admits, for argument sake, our road would secure part of the lumber and minerals, and asks, 'Would not the carriage of this heavy produce constantly wear out the cheap, light rails?' Certainly; and the more the merrier. Have they got everlasting rails on the Lindsay road?

"The rules of proportion in engineering science will not be violated by the Engineers who construct the cheap railroad to Gull River, and their reports to the committee will more authoritatively settle the question.

"It is alleged by 'Observer' that the railroad at present in operation is capable of doing the business of the county for the next thirty years, but at the rate of present progress, aided by a new railway, two or three new counties will be added to the civilized area of the country north-eastward before that date expires; and if twenty lines of road to Gull River would not take a 'twentieth part from the Port Hope line in either passengers or freight,' there is then no reason to fear such a very little road as is modestly proposed, which, however, your friend admits, 'would doubtless secure the grain traffic from the townships through which it ran,' which is satisfactory.

"The resolutions carried by the committee, and sent to all the municipal authorities on the route of 'our road,' asking for information, absolve me from the charge of wittingly 'misleading people;' but the answers of the above-mentioned and competent authorities may furnish satisfactory reasons for retorting your correspondent's uncharitable suspicions.

"Your obedient servant,

"Toronto, March 25, 1867. "G. LAIDLAW."

Printed by Libri Plureos GmbH in Hamburg, Germany